HEERA: MY PRECIOUS DIAMOND

A BOUQUET OF ARTY POEMS

FIROZ TATA (WOLFY)

Dedicating to the most precious woman of my life whom I love with all my heart and soul more than anyone on the planet. She is none other than my beloved mummy Ms. Heera Minoo Tata.

Without her I wouldn't have learnt how true love looks and feels like. Thank you mummy for everything you have done for me/us.

Yours forever loving son,

Fillu

Contents

Author's Note

Dear Readers,

Although the note from the author or the preface is the first part of the book that you read, it is the last part that I prefer to write for my readers. I am very fortunate to observe and feel the world around me, deeply experience emotions and memorize interesting events that can cook up into captivating poetries, quotes as well as stories. By relishing the gradual process of writing as much as I did in my initial years, I sincerely hope to give long-lasting reading pleasure to my ever-growing circle of local as well as overseas readers.

Once again a burning desire towards writing and a deep passion for poetries helped me to create this book during the most challenging phase of my life. Just after two days of creating nine of these poems (while my mother was already unwell) a heart-shattering truth I discovered. On 30th September 2022 my mother got diagnosed with a very serious life threatening illness. However, time came where I had no other option but to be the Wolfy of the strongest self to face reality and protect her at any cost. To my bottled-up anger and extreme sorrow my mother landed in this dreadful situation due to the initial medical negligence and ignorance of the primary doctors as we were kept in the dark, (based on her health history) while avoiding any further medical investigations although she had gradually started to show symptoms for nearly six months. The retribution on the judgement day of trusting the wrong so very right is sweeter and less sinful than first stealing someone's confidence and brutally assaulting it, playing with the innocent body and later committing a betrayal. However, with God's grace, she is now in the safest hands and a very experienced and dedicated team of doctors. Back to the book, my craving and endless hunger to visualize and absorb more and more has always helped me to discover various poetic themes that are close to my heart and more or less related to my very simple, distant from the people and not so interesting life.

Although my heart cries and soul aches for my mother, I feel blessed in bringing out to you a bouquet of 12 artistic poems by placing into your hands, 'Heera: My Precious Diamond' a book that I have named after her. In times of uncertainty and unpredictability, I fell in love to pen down my sincere frame of mind in the form of stanzas, coining into beautiful poems. I am confident that these poems will help in creating vivid and spectacular visions in your minds and hearts. The book possesses a unique sight of a creative mind that has cautiously shaped and integrated the lines that seem ordinary but are an extraordinary symphony of different intellectual colours.

Creating a poem is indeed the labour of long hours and immense brainstorming. Precise vocabulary and rhyming words are the influential tools through which one can depict their innermost reflection of self, soul and emotions. I too have tried my best to express myself through various poignant, happy, educational as well as inspirational verses. Special efforts are made to select appropriate expressions making all poems coherent in their reading and understanding. I am certain that this book will not only touch the minds and hearts of the readers, but will also enrich their souls and lives in general. Moreover, the handsome blending of vocabulary will surely capture your attention, as it will spread freshness much like a refreshing dawn delighting several hearts.

Poems have always helped me to tranquilize some of the deepest thoughts and anxieties that keep circling in my head. Before beginning the journey of creating this book, little was I aware of the fact that testing times were just round the corner that could exhaust every ounce of me; mentally, physically and financially. However, writing poems not only helped me to vent out my views through stanzas, but also helped me to get into the shoes of several others who might not have got an opportunity to express what they feel within their innermost selves. Hence, I believe, this book will help in sharpening and augmenting the ingenious horizons of the readers. It will also educate them to express their feelings and opinions confidently. Let me assure you that this publication will go a very long way in increasing the liking for poems and further assist in developing a writing flair. I have no doubt that this book will be welcomed as a moving experience for all, especially for literature and poetry lovers.

Finally, yet importantly, I feel great happiness to make my readers know that the interior and the cover page of the book is designed by myself with the help of a beautiful Interior Formatting Tool and Cover Creator provided by the Notion Press publishers. It has always been challenging, learning and a wonderful experience altogether. I am confident that I will continue to create more poems in future and my readers too will keenly welcome my writings as always. With these words, I take great honour and privilege in unlocking yet another door of the Wolfy's world of poetries.

Hey, lads and lasses, uncles and aunties of all ages; don't forget to spread your million-dollar smile after reading my poetries. Kindly, without fail share your valuable reviews on **reviewmypublications@gmail.com.**

I sincerely request all my readers to pray for my mother and keep sending good wishes for her speedy recovery and a very long and healthy life. Amen!

Love, respect and take care of your mother every day, before it gets too late.

- The Author

(Mumbai)

Acknowledgements

I share my words of acknowledgement and heartfelt gratitude to my loving and sacrificing mother Ms. Heera Minoo Tata. As a son, I express my earnest care and love to her. She has always been my strongest supporter no matter what. Each time she has raised my spirit and unconditionally encouraged me during my highs and lows in my several writing journeys.

I also extend my sincere acknowledgement to Notion Press publishers for providing a platform of Xpress Publishing through which my 25th book is published for sales in India as well as overseas.

Finally and importantly, I also want to thank every single one of you who has stuck with me since the last 15 years of my writing journey.

1. Dear Mummy

Birthing a fetal macrosomia into the world's doorstep,
Overlooking your atrocious agonies at the sidestep.
Sacrificing your mind, body, heart and soul,
Kept on walking; to keep me safe from burning coal.
You were, are and will always be there as my Christ,
Dear mummy, you are the one whom I love the most.

During your currently critical life's ride I'll express,
My precious diamond, I'll keep cherishing and well-care.
I'll love and guard you like a tame-wild Wolfy,
Dear mummy, I again thank Him to bestow you upon me.

Although limited material things and time we possess,
I promise, the eternal bond we value and share will never get less.
The colossal might will struggle to fall mother-son apart,
As our fragrant love will bloom even in our dead hearts.
Dear mummy, you are my only angel blessed to never depart.

2. Guru

Unfortunately I hate to write great for most of them,
Shaped me, shall ever be grateful to that one gem.
Never strove for means, material and name,
Taught me the basis, igniting a success flame.

My unsung, unknown and forever lost hero,
Toiled on a dumb mind, instilling education to a zero.
Abilities and attainments easy to be distinguished,
Respect and love of numerous students she cherished.

Changed my life for good; gradually forever,
Brushed the ignorance with knowledge so clever.
Created a craving to learn more and more,
Kindled the spark within, to fight every life-war.

Be blessed with peace, praise and strength,
Be bestowed with prosperity, health and wealth.
My childhood's treasured bliss,
She is none other than my guru Prakash miss.

3. A Voice Within

That voice within to make the correct choice,

When circled by qualms and dismay,

Helping to keep the pessimism at bay.

Hearing this teeny voice,

He will be the guiding light.

Earnest praying to engross in Him,

The more one grows within,

The more one moves towards a new beginning.

They indulge in greed, distrust, arrogance and egoism,

Though born to spread generosity, trust, humility and altruism.

That voice within lights through several tasks,

He guides us, only if we unmask.

Commotion, clash and conflict bound,

Less joy and more pain all around.

Troubles and lures everywhere,

Deceitful hands scare and stare.

They trap and tangle,

Making feeble during the struggle.

When we fail; we question why?

We must stand up and fight.

Fib and false fantasies day and night,

Let that voice within strongly ignite.

Though igniting it; adversity may befall,

Never lose peace, steering through the storm with ease.

The path ahead paved tricky yet bright,
Well lit by His lively light.
There would remain no cause for fear,
As heavenly hands will be always near.

4. A Ride Called Life

A ride called life we undertake,
Full of right and wrong choices we make.
A path that often seems dark and vague,
An uncertain map throughout the life-voyage.

Sunrise, sunburn, sunset and repeat,
Some pleasure and so often pain heat.
Shame, sorrow and a few unknown fears,
Who will rescue and wipe our tears?

A ride called life so enthralling,
Tremors, treachery and trauma at each turning.
Every dark night has a certain ending,
Every fresh dawn brings a new beginning.

Life's windy winds storm us left and right,
Clutching tight away from the destination fight.
Accomplishing the goal a big trial and test,
Covering the distance with some rest and full zest.

Knowing the place; holding His caring hand,
Firm faith in Him, will surely reach the vowed land.
Acknowledging Him for His unconditional divinity,
His love and miracles will keep augmenting our sanity.

A ride called life; a platform to be drilled,
Changing obstacles into occasions fruitfully achieved.
One's life a mansion created by Him,
Virtuous decisions spreading ecstasy and glim.

Immortal souls treasured in mortal bodies,
A day inscribed when one dies.
The heavenly spark carrying the soul,
Forever to its righteous side.

5. Sympathy

Sympathy is kindness and affection for all,
Be His creations big or small.
An attribute that blesses both; giver and taker,
Making life less grim, giving hope when things flicker.
Loving one another and feeling the pain of others,
Selfless help, healing the unhappy brothers and sisters.
Compassion is what we also call,
Care, respect and love for all.
An ability to witness ray of hope in the dark,
Igniting within a courageous spark.
Someone suffering wrapped in shame and pain,
Sympathetic hand, to help him rise again.
Show sympathy to the deserving one and all,
Making this planet a gorgeous huge hall.
Almighty all above is surely watching us,
Waiting to reward us, thus.

6. No Task That Cannot be Undertaken

Once every human arrives a dissuasive moment,
What will be the course of action for attainment?
Pondering wisely, hearing the deepest instincts,
Urging towards those steps, leading to victory.

Deciding to follow the guidance of that final guide,
Shall be no sorrows, only victorious strides.
The path may appear bumpy and challenging,
For every problem exists an undiscovered bridging.

When the journey starts to meet its end,
The task will turn much easier, the soul will ascend.
Be strong and enduring,
Facing days with new hope-twinkling.
Well-lit within an immense faith unshaken,
There remains no task that cannot be undertaken.

7. He

Conversing with Him through purity of prayers,
Meditating in silence, healing our scars and wiping tears.
Self-enlightening with prayers and meditation, never losing our way,
Created with a purpose; teaching, testing and guiding every day.

Unshaken faith and sincere bond,
He will safely swim us through the life-pond.
Anxiety and stress will be cut-short,
Only if one walks on His righteous path.

Keeping life-ethics high and clear,
There remains no want to fear, my dear.
Good words, good thoughts and good deeds;
A stepping stone towards sanity, leading to eternity.

He who has formed us for the worldly halt,
Directing and diminishing the burden of salt.
Cares and loves all that He created,
Prosperity of the beautiful world He decorated.

8. Joy

Joy is a choice and a state of mind,
The more we chase, the harder to find.
More we share, more it stays,
More it stays, the more we can multiply,
Keeping most problems at bay.

Despair dusts thundering around,
Take shelter under His colossal crown.
Blues blistering and overwhelming us,
And when no hope and cheer prevails,
Trust Him, He will wind in our sails.

When things seem to be not alright,
Emerging the strength awaking the asleep might.
Warmth and comfort from the inner light,
He will certainly reduce our plight,
Never lose hope and quit the fight.

Learning to see every good in others,
Raise human deeds, dear brothers and sisters.
Good thoughts and words guiding us,
We will improve our spiritual worth.
Joy is an expensive flower; not affordable by all,
Value its rare existence; whether big or small.

Clouds of sadness blurring our vision,
Train the mind towards inner diversion.
Seeking the light from Him,
Paving the prosperous path, ripping the dark,
Dispersing the fragrance spark.

9. Education

Education paves the path towards virtuous life,
Prepares us with vital tools to tackle the strife.
Frames the personality; creating mentally cognitive,
Teaches us to be modest, gratified and expressive.
Magnifies the vision; refines the speech,
Reflecting through behaviour, introspection it teaches.
Learning from the mistakes; pursuing the truth,
Education empowers youth to choose the correct route.

Making each hurdle easy,
Gaining profits and fame,
Avoiding being inept and clumsy.
Not all, but surely a few great teachers,
Outwardly stern, nurturing the young saplings,
Budding them into fruity trees.
Constantly carry on their noble task,
For material rewards they do not ask.
Attention and respect all they desire,
Enduring-walk on the righteous path through fire.

Education is a journey that lasts lifelong,
Helps in testing times, with learning all along.
It is a change of thoughts in words and then into deeds,
Only accumulation of facts will not help one to succeed.

A challenging world with stresses and strains,
Keep working sustaining inner peace, defeating the pains.
A gift of an education; is the best we can offer,
Not allowing anyone to stay duffer.
Thus, the more one gains wisdom,
The more life becomes a prosperous kingdom.

10. Problems

Problems can make us wise and strong,
Frowning and grumbling is very wrong.
When they troop up and stand,
Struggle and change them into a victory garland.

Accept the situation and never play a blame-game,
Analyze and work hard, making your problems lame.
Storming through hurdles and burnt bridges,
Why get upset and hold any grudges?

Optimistic approach; facing problems with a grin,
Gradually working on and throwing them in a trash bin.
Causes a temporary sadness and setback,
Hiding and escaping from them is a drawback.

Learn to deal with the wrong that crosses your path,
Discovering the right is the actual growth.
Be sincere and firm believer in His grace,
Will bring inner solace and ahead in every race.
Pessimism consuming our energy within,
Trust me, they will vanish like a thief from the crime scene.

11. Hopes

Once love knocked hard at my heart's door.
Wasn't easy to fake and soon let it in,
Had an ample vacant space residing her within.

Giving his burnt wings a faith of golden swing,
A pride to let them know her wild heart's musical ding.

Never self-seeking, never easily irate,
Past of wounds, healing for a peaceful fate.

Always exhaled truth, inhaled trust, shielding the other,
Two hearts hanging alive finding divine hope-ray further.
Still pumping on certain hopeful instincts for one another.

12. Before it's too Late

If someone, we aren't talking,
Had only a few hours before leaving.
What would we say?
No point in waiting,
When those few hours have started end-racing.

Storming emotions in which we drawn,
When somebody we madly love lets us down.
Moments and memories repetitive in mind,
We fail to accept why they were unkind.
Was this worth it in the end?

Words are left unspoken,
Hours turn into weeks.
Before we realize months turn into mountains.
We hold on to something for years.
How would we feel if the end was near?

Imagine how a best buddy felt,
Not speaking to that friend over something petty,
Being told their friend passed away, sleeping on a settee.
Imagine how a son felt,
Upset with his parents, not saying, "I love you back",
Only to find out they perished on a railway track.

If reading this brought someone special into your mind,
Tell that person how you feel until life is little kind.
While there is still some time,
Make your life a sweet chime.
Life is too short and regret can be too long.
How will you feel when that person is gone?

Perhaps reading this poem was fate.
Tell that person how you really feel,
Before it's too late!
Before it's too late!

About The Author

FIROZ TATA (Wolfy) is a non-practicing priest, an author, a poet, notion creator, a storyteller and a national level cyclist from Mumbai, India. He is credited to win several prestigious medals and trophies in the sport of cycling. He has been fascinating his nationwide readers with his academic as well as fictional writings for nearly 15 years.

He has shown his strong writing influence through informative and imaginative essays, instructive letters, heart-warming poems, engrossing stories and captivating quotes depicting resolve, love, women, beauty, life and hopes. However, he is a single man, perhaps patiently waiting for someone. He firmly believes to love and to be loved loyally and passionately from a distance rather than sticking in an intolerable and suffocative relationship.

Due to his deserted, suppressive and cut off childhood and adolescent years from the outer world, he had no other alternative but to develop a deep passion and skills for writing since his early days. Back then, as a child, he was destined to encounter numerous terrible experiences with his several teachers. He also had his share of horrible experiences at home that no child deserves.

After failing miserably in English in the last and decisive year of his schooling, no one but only him through the burning desire, dedication and determination in his heart knew that one day he would become a published author. Years later, he successfully did. Even today, he is dedicated to the path of enriching himself with knowledge and improving with the passing years.

By now, he has authored nearly 60 academic as well as fictional books for various publishers. His works also include nearly 500 essays and 800 quotes in his total 17 creative writing books. His books are strongly recommended not only for the bookshelves of children, but also adults. His works are highly appreciated and acclaimed by several readers, educationalists and publishers.

This and many other books written by Firoz Tata (Wolfy) are
available on the publisher's website notionpress.com
(With read instant feature), on national and international Amazon sites
in paperback and Kindle formats and also on flipkart.com
Kindly share your valuable reviews and suggestions on
reviewmypublications@gmail.com
Those readers interested in joining Wolfy Books WhatsApp group,
kindly send an email on the above given email address.